# rectangle

# 구형

# sun

# 태양

# turtle

터틀

ten

십

# car

차

# ear

귀

# strawberry

딸기

six

여섯

# home

집

# pig

돼지

# bread

빵

# cherry

체리

# apple

# 사과

circle

원

star

별

# kangaroo

# 캥거루

# cat

# 고양이

# toy

# 장난감

# giraffe

기린

# tree

나무

# snail

# 달팽이

# bed

# 침대

# crab

게

# table

# spider

# 거미

# monkey

# 원숭이

# owl

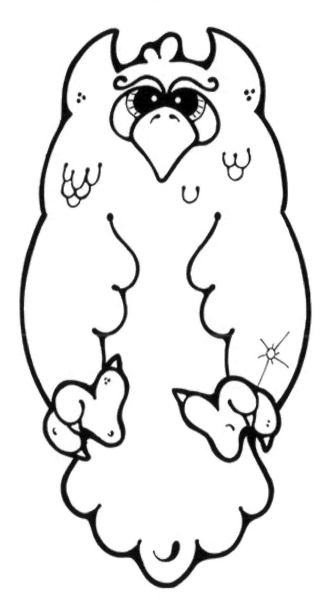

# 올빼미

# cheetah

# 치타

one

하나

# COW

소

# lobster

랍스터

deer

사슴

# hamster

햄스터

# frog

# 개구리

# bee

벌

# chimpanzee

침팬지

two

둘

# boy

# 소년

# triangle

삼각형

# grape

포도

# camel

낙다

# worm

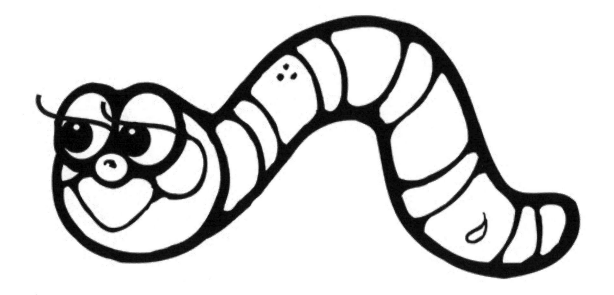

# 벌레

# shark

# 상어

# panda

팬더

# fish

# 물고기

# squirrel

# 다람쥐

# lion

# 사자

# bathtub

# 목욕통

# sheep

양

five

다섯

eye

ᅡᄂ

# seal

# 봉인

square

광장

# butterfly

나비

# watermelon

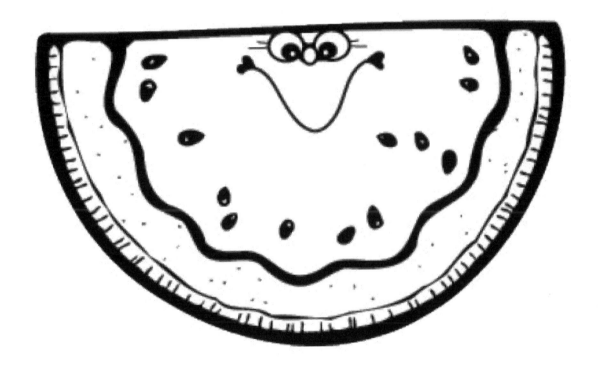

수박

# snake

뱀

# alligator

악어

# eagle

# 독수리

# bear

곰

# eight

여덟

# rabbit

토끼

four

# goat

# 염소

# orange

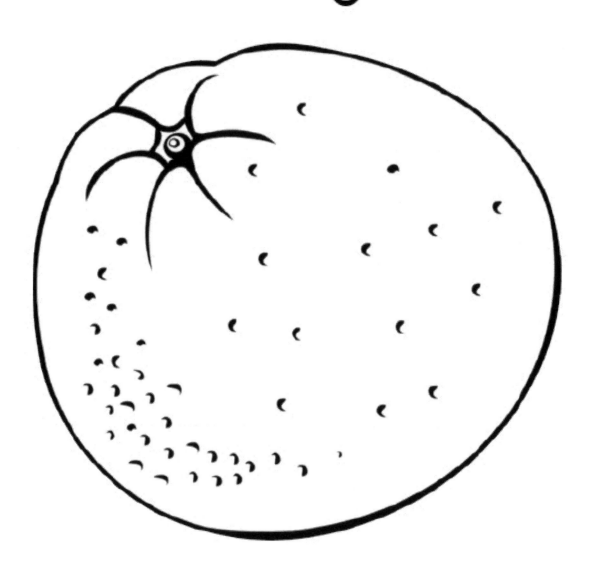

# 주황색

# horse

말

ladder

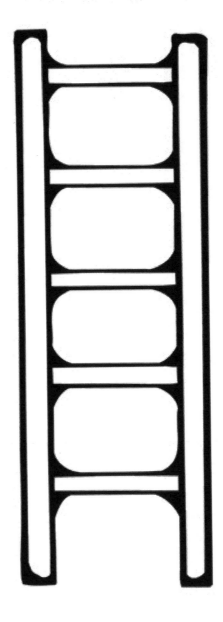

사닥다리

# goldfish

# 금붕어

# hippopotamus

하마

# dragonfly

# 잠자리

# duck

# 오리

# three

세

nine

아홉

# girl

소녀

# teacher

선생

rat

쥐

# wolf

# 늑대

# zero

제 로

# tiger

호랑이

# fox

여우

# seven

# 일곱

# water

물

# elephant

# 코끼리

dog

개

# pear

배

# chair

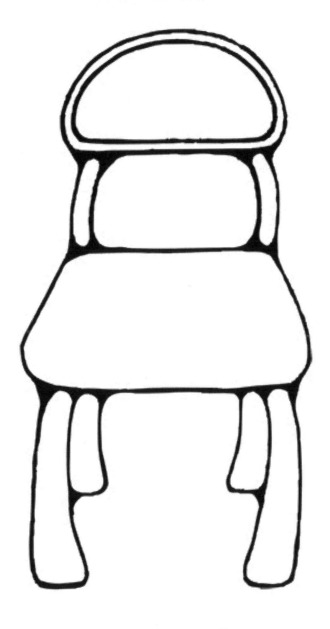

# 의자

# moon

달

# dolphin

# 돌고래

# book

책

# dinosaur

# 공룡

# ship

배

# hair

# 머리

# cloud

# 구름

# banana

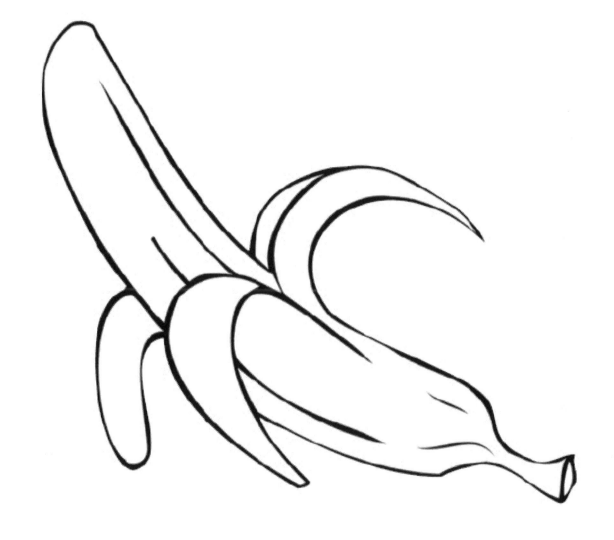

바나나

# bird

새

milk

우유

# octopus

# 문어

# chicken

# 치킨

# zebra

# 얼룩말

# ant

# 개미

oval

타원

47343104R00057

Made in the USA
Middletown, DE
06 June 2019

ISBN 9781097918188